salmonpoetry

An Unfinished Sufficiency

Ruth O'Callaghan

salmonpoetry

Published in 2015 by
Salmon Poetry
Cliffs of Moher, County Clare, Ireland
Website: www.salmonpoetry.com
Email: info@salmonpoetry.com

Copyright © Ruth O'Callaghan, 2015

ISBN 978-1-910669-04-4

All rights reserved. No part of this publication may be reproduced or transmitted in any form or by any means, electronic or mechanical, including photography, recording, or any information storage or retrieval system, without permission in writing from the publisher. The book is sold subject to the condition that it shall not, by way of trade or otherwise, be lent, resold or otherwise circulated without the publisher's prior consent in any form of binding or cover other than that in which it is published and without a similar condition, including this condition, being imposed on the subsequent purchaser.

COVER PHOTOGRAPHY: *Jessie Lendennie*
COVER DESIGN & TYPESETTING: *Siobhán Hutson*
Printed in Ireland by Sprint Print

for Chris
Without whose love and encouragement
this book would never have happened

Acknowledgements

Acknowledgements and thanks are due to the editors of the following magazines:

Acumen, Agenda, Brittle Star, Critical Survey, Dreamcatcher, Envoi, French Literary Review, Gunu (Mongolia) *Magma, Mobius* (USA), *Pro Saeculum* (Romania), *The SHOp.*

Sincere apologies if any magazine has been inadvertently omitted.

Contents

Edges

A Calculation of Dark	11
Without Compass	12
Whereupon	14
Reservoir	15
Passage	16
Safari	19
Caravan	20
Of No Tomorrow	26
2.53 p.m.	27
Villanelle	28
The dark	29
…perhaps	30
Stopping Place	31
Outside	32

Spaces in a Journey

Incidents in the Travels of an Itinerant Cellist	35
Awakening	38
Debut	39
Birthright	40
It isn't	41
For Mary	42
Bury your own dead	43
What is left	44
Perspective	45
North Circular	47
O'Shea Is Granted Enlightenment Outside Fantasy Nails, Boston, Massachusetts	48

Histories

Narrative	51
Vasilije: Christmas Eve	52
Josif	53
The Re-Telling	54
Aftermath	59
Appetites	60
Ghazal	61
Ghazal: In Situ	62
Black Bandanna	63
The Collection	64
Alterations	65
Acceptance	66
On Our 60th Anniversary	67
Histories	68
Subsequent	69

Dismantling the Margins

Shaping the poem	73
Punctuation	74
Investigate	75
What....	78
Oblique...	79
Coalition...	80
Concentration........	81
To Whom It May Concern	82

Edges

A Calculation of Dark

In this ruined light – the dark leaking into the garden
as if light were an interloper

whose presence, no longer desired,
is sequestered to other places – the urgency of shadow

conspires, determines cross-woven words that lie
in the gap between desire

and undisclosed restraints.
Such absence is mocked by the *schack-schack* of jay

concealed in the elderberry beyond the boundary wall
but a quiver of leaves betrays

as will a breath, caught,
or the silk-split of a leaf loosed from its stem.

Without Compass

A gull struts
feet more gristle than flesh
            imprint an ideograph

where waves whimper
chafing the sand
to reclaim its own.

Each year this house
concupiscent, eases
its grip. The cliff crumbling.

Below
the town dark, dressed in night rain
retains its own
            terrible privacy.

Only a drumming silence
— as when a room is entered
            unexpectedly

the room empty
though the air alive
         with out-of-earshot rustle
words fretting the door —
a discord of motes
            implicates

        the way a glance
over a shoulder in field or wood
           the light
                  slant

      glimpses   a form

merging in the tree's leaf
the oak hanging acorns
catkins spangled from willow

                                              nothing
to substantiate dissidence
except the unmap of the lost
                        their voices wittering
a noose of roots and knotweed underfoot.

Whereupon

What absence we sought in the loose
weave of light and shadow, eluded.

We could only wait out the long burn
of winter, each feeling the weight

of weather, folding each into himself
denying the sly making of small miracles.

Cocooned, we did not know whose grief
we held or who would listen to our plaint.

Mute, we only knew brute omission left
absence harder to bear than scourge

of stone: the fig-and-nettle broth of lies
that followed loss, hollowed grief to a reed.

Reservoir

Water thin glass
defies the dark

the room lit
by a bowl of white anemones

one petal smears an old book
imprint unknown

lying closed beside
the photograph whose memory

she refutes when, at the still
of approaching rain

shelter is sought.
in the fall of unpainted hills.

Passage

We did not know what or who
or why. We only knew.

In that long heat nothing was said
but it hung there

a pinioned crow
for other birds to savage.

Not, as you may suppose
the larger kind but small

sparrows, starlings.
Then there was the thrush.

It's song halted in the pecking.
That remained as unspoken

as where we'd meet each night
once released from our summer jobs

but somehow we'd drift together
first one then another tagging on

aware-unaware
to loaf along the riverbank

where a swan drowned
entangled in a fisherman's cast-offs.

Later, after the last bell-ringer had left
we'd huddle in the churchyard

the night still
still with August heat in the crushed grass

that stained our clothes
or lay with marble cool on our back

where a tee had ridden up.
The marble had its own cold urgency

had names in gold lettering.
We'd trail fingertips

pretend we couldn't see
touch each separate part

trace each curve.
To make letters come alive

the boys said
we need a living model

with a firm stroke, flattering
innocent Eugenie

who wore black
I ♥ Gravy

emblazoned across her chest.
Eugenie, anxious to please

sang the letters in duet with Rodney.
Was it that night

of that last summer with all those
floating-under-glass feelings

we moved towards reality?
Towards the mute acceptance

in October
of the burser emptying Eugenie's locker

of the boys, silent and serious
as men now

and Rodney, small and feral
deciding not to be a rock icon

to join Featherstone and Steele
Loss Adjusters.

That summer
the stang of fox was ever-present.

Safari

I have left linen bleaching in a white sun
by an inlet with its slack of winter water

where a heron breaks free from brittle light.
Skin tightened with cold desires the code

of touch. Unregarded, the curvature of trees
bears the mark of previous snows, grass

shrivelled, the earth bitten: winter-ravenous.
Winter-ravenous, I will arrive: my feet bare.

Caravan

Were we other
    we would be a
        single
        straight
        line of camels
        stringing the horizon

      humps bulging or diminished
                      depending
in the quest for water
if thirst had been
  slaked.

A serai would be
            appended
yet here
    different appendages apply

    chains
    sunk
into concrete
against inclement weather.

            There is leeway
    but not as saplings
always bending to the wind.

Rocked by the heaviest storm
            still we hold fast
            content now
              not

to drain the day's full measure
              but

to return
to fold into ourselves
to small pleasures
to knowing

that in them
each minute has yielded its own full stretch.

                                  Beyond the window
— the cliffs too high to hear the sea —
                                      a kayak
the paddle flaying the waves
as if pursued by voices
                by the raconteur of land.
The sea
holds its own consummate might
                                but

with the wash of water
healing salt
   tends
the wound
                        — actual or imagined —

that denies the mind's quiet
              turning
                    in
on itself.
          Contained.

  We are contained
                        in this caravan
                the pinch and ease of it

compact
 in its entirety
all space utilitarian, storage

                    all unwanted matter
                          contained

            as we edge
            awake

a hint of damp ever-present.

Rain thrums the roof
yet the skin will hold fast
no tear, no rent
              despite gulls skid-padding in
              despite their ready-made runway
                    for take-off.

                                  We will follow.
                                  We will leave
the light blaring our small window
the seethe of rain lifted
                    exposing
                              the shingle spit
                              the rip
alive with seal pup— December born —
                        their small grey faces
                            expectant
                            expectant too

the waves
        furling
      unfurling
the way the surge and ebb of grief
                            engulfs the body

the way it does now
with those seals that are other
                            summer-bearing.

The grunt and wrestle of delivery
precludes males
                bringing with it
the jealous watchguard of motherhood
                              the fire in the eye

when a camera-click of ferry
                    drifts too close.
Aboard
      an old woman gnaws
              the cone's last tapering
              her tongue seeking sweetness
              her gums mumbling the ice.
Above
      the sky grey with gulls
              gull-grey also the sand
                      shifting
            the way the old
                  shift
                          an easing
of the years' weight
          the light slant and the eye opaque.

Owen
     fifty years on this coast
     sixty if you count the boy
     unable to handle the river
alone
            releases his hand on the tiller.

Tomorrow

                he will take the weight of his father
                      on his shoulder
the step slow
the ground infirm
from the slur of water.

He will set the coffin
of the oldest river-man
to guide the rudder

                    for a final circle
                    of the seals.

Deference demands the river boat-empty
the quarrel of gulls quietened
the stars exact
            himself uncompassed

yet to learn
      the mastery of tears
                  or how silence floods a crowded room.

Tomorrow
a bell will toll
  binding
the old man
to those who ventured beyond
                      before

their nails rimed with salt
hands slippy with entrails
            with fish, blood fringing the gills
their slither of words
                sensate.

                        They knew
                            the power and innocence
of steel
the belly slit
the limit of red.

                        In the bones
an ancient knowledge
of quartering
of the stench of flesh
                        fire melting fat
the crowd waiting
while the skin crisps.

    The last gull
         pegs a fish
the lights of the last bus hurry our steps.

Serrated wrack strews the beach
causing us to stumble.
                  You slip
                  your arm into the crook of mine
encompassing the day
                      an unfinished sufficiency.

Of No Tomorrow

Was it summer we strolled in Grbavica, sat in the square
alight with fireflies, returned each night to strip

fish from bones, drink Slivovice from small glasses, the toss
of hands growing faster and faster before fumbling

back to our unmade bed, lips black from wine?
Waking to windows smoky in sunlight, hair straggling

a thigh and the sour smell of love?
Yet still we laughed while a laze of bees drowsed the days.

In lemon groves, the sharp of citrus in our throats or, tongues
salty with love on a spread of beach, we played

with doe-eyed boys. Harsh with hope we over-spent days –
September sun showed scavenging crows in ravaged fields.

Summer's faces retreated to the discreet of a dark that could not
erase the bruise of words, the past remained in grained photos,

albums on which to map memories. We turned leaves
but autumn failed us: sap-less trees in deserted streets.

2.53 p.m.

Day-dark. Small evidences of winter's advance:
sheen-wet of trees when no rain has fallen,
the wind voicing the grief of reeds, a rope
of small birds seek shelter from unresolved light,
their song diminished. Only the ache of hope
in the lone dunnock's cry splices the cold air.

Villanelle

Moving towards morning yet still the still night
layers the air, holds close the shutter,
allows no possibility of light.

Even desire, whose secret threads, folded tight,
escapes in night's cries, dies in mutters
moving towards morning. Yet still the still night

persists, pursues, caresses, seeks to ignite –
but as candles, denied air, gutter,
allow no possibility of light,

so desire, held in its own heat, burns to spite
and words of love remain unuttered
moving towards morning. Yet still the still night

hungers in unlit rooms where even contrite
prayers quavered behind locked doors, stutter,
allow no possibility of light.

Some desire desire as love yet when such slight
hope fades then nothing remains only, eyes half-shut,
moving towards morning. Yet still the still night
allows no possibility of light.

The dark

angles inwards,
forms ancient ruts
on landscapes untouched
by the tableaux
of skulls easing
beneath the hollowed berg:

it curves fear,
manoeuvres space and night
into shifting havens:
laughs at the clapping
in distant graveyards.

...perhaps

                    unsettled
the dark unlit

a pebble loosened
a step without
              purchase

or a sigh   hanging
in winter-air

              discards

as a sweep of rain
will cleanse the day

Stopping Place

Our eyes sly-slitted against a low sun
our wheels waist high
                      we devoured dust
scrub that gave way to cactii
trees and a ring of rocks
                          the boundaries of wolves.

We had learnt never to stop
even though the cab filled with his farts and the air
filled with the burnt warmth from the engine that lay
                                          between us
smothered with cloth

even though the rope-rigging
                loosened
and the load began to shift and slide.

Where the valley narrowed
bone-white littered.
                            Skulls. Some
ascertainable as cattle. Passing others
                                        more familiar
we crossed ourselves, gave thanks for deliverance

but kept our eyes road-wise
    kept the cab close-closed against
                        the cries of the slope-backed
old woman gathering slats, her home the four miles
we'd cover before her curses ended
                before the light's silvering
of olive trees, the fruit weathered.

In the shape-shift of garden
the well without a handle
                      buried secrets
                        deep
                        black
                        blank
                        to the eye.

Outside

There were edges to that world, margins never trod, and spaces in a journey where absence lingered weathering the frame. Fingers that knew no cold traced rain tatting on windows. The boneless words of a child, indistinct, quivers as the lamp spills its light on a book, open, the page unturned: the Paschal candle removed.

Spaces in a Journey

Incidents in the Travels of an Itinerant Cellist

Fahey believes he is Samson Agonistes
                                                  with a cello
that'll rival the horsehead fiddles of Mongolia when he humps it
                                                  across the Gobi

giving a nod to Bogdkhan, Tsagaan Nuur and even
       the Darkhad Depression
before its mellow tones bring a smile to Chinngis seated
                                     in Sükhbaatar Square.

Fahey knows,
       having consulted the world wide web @ shaggyyak,
                        that courtesy is key
and is prepared to accept the proffered vodka at whatever time,

morning, noon, or,
                      but preferably *and*, night, will offer in return
Mal sureg targan tavtai uu?* and a comment on the *khavtgai*.**

He's a tad uncertain about the consumption
                                of blowtorched marmot:
                          knowing the bubonic
is in the handling of their skins in August and September

he'll arrive in July to be on the safe side — being, at the moment,
                                            in transit,
                                            in Belgium.

Next to the Manneken Pis Fahey straddles his cello naked
                                           of thought.
Petite Angelique has passed the hat but tourists are blind
                                         to her blandishments,

deaf to the instrument's resonance, attending only to their guide
                                      flaunting his floral umbrella
tied to its purple ribbon, in this labyrinthine city where shades

                                              stalk
                                        the ornamental
                                           in the park
and Hades lies, as Hades must, in the guise of a building
                                          with many stars.

Petite Angelique has led her lover to the Grand' Place. Beneath
her gothic façade she loves to explore the baroque delights
                                        of many layered
                                            petticoats
                                  the pout of too-pink lips,

the play of light and shade on inner thigh.
In a secret recess she carries Caravaggio.
                        He kisses her behind with every step.
Behind her with every step Fahey curses

Purcell,
        his cello,
                Petite Angelique's lover
whose 5 p.m. stubble sprouts under foundation and powder-pink.

Fahey lusts
        for the chink, ker-chink of coinage. He has travelled so far:
                                              so far
the cents do not amount to a single euro: he dreads a repetition
                                of the Athenian expedition.

At the exact spot
                that architecte extraordinaire
                Jan von Ruysbroeck landed.
Fahey attempts to transport himself beyond this Place,
                                beyond the eternal quest

for cents and silver, to return to those hallowed days of hangovers
                                              and hymns
                                     in the college chapel.

Fahey mourns
                      baguettes and berets,
              the citizens social charter,
remembers this is Belgium: pigeons and Manneken Pis.
Fahey knows suicide is one option, thrown from the top
                                  like Jan von.

A light rain spatters Fahey who wrestles to cover his cello,
                                  resolves to travel
only with a penny whistle if ever he can redeem his reputation.

Dusk. Whispers infiltrate the parc,
        eclipse the earlier call of boys practising moves
showing patience beyond their years as their friend perfects

        the shoulder roll,
        the double flick-twist,
        the double feint
to throw the pursuer, to retain the ball at all costs.
        To pursue a new goal.

Fahey rejects the overtures of M'sieu Lambeaux
                      whose major in Japanese Gothic
allows him to conduct impassioned diatribes on the haut-relief
            of the Human Passions;

his designs to re-vamp the grand but dusty artefacts
                have been sketched by petite Angelique
whose minor gothic movements Fahey prefers. Fahey knows
                              he and his cello
                                need
                                to leave
                                this city.

* Are your sheep fattening up nicely?
** wild camels.

Awakening

Dawn did not creep through this empty land
arising from a far horizon suddenly near
the sky flamboyant, the steppe a blue dazzle
blinding even the most carefully hooded eye.

Butterflies frazzle in such unexpected light
a startled gazelle seeks cooler climes, leaps
north, swerves west, is drawn inevitably east
where ibex lock backward curving horns.

Argali sheep hidden by rocks watch eagles
swoop on the dazed, too long in hibernation
woken by the clamour, vulnerable in light.
Black kites wait by the wayside, inscrutable.

Debut

The stars have determined the date
of his acknowledgement, known even
before the empty year, the womb-warm
nine months his mother carried him,

accounting it the first of life. He stands,
sturdy as a gyr pole, in the finest deel
afforded by the family, a khadig held tighter
than a pony's reins, the blue cloth receiving

each clipped lock, his head caressed
by many hands – respected guest, elder –
each offering a bleating lamb or kid,
his first husbandry, his first hair cut.:

the first three years terminated by parents
solemnly shaving the small head yet careful
to leave a single lock to honour Ayurzana:
grandfather, ancient, significant, absent.

Birthright

Ayurzana Luvsandamba prepares to shave his head. He will keep
the old ways of the blue-haze steppe where he gathered dung,
crumbling pats, flung haphazard, missing the wicker strapped
to his back, stumbling over uneven ground that is his birthright.
He knew tears sharp as stones before mastering each art of life
yet he would be master
                        ...but not of the woman whom he chose
for a wife, the one who would not braid her black hair, wearing it
loose as she flew across the turf, reins careless, her teeth bared
against a wind that bore the smell of wolf. Ayurzana Luvsandamba
remembers the wail of his mother naming others he could marry:

girls who would place stones deep to heat in the tall pot, layering
meat and bones, potato, carrot, more stones: girls who would milk
sheep, goats, yaks, smoke camel meat, offer arak to strangers
seeking shelter, girls who would stitch thirty-six intricate patterns
on their bridal boots but the woman he chose wore her boots plain,

the turned up toes protecting soil where no blood may be spilled.
This woman burned days, returned the wolf's night howl, came
to him in the moonlit gyr, covering breasts with her pelt of hair,
her touch soft as cashmere as she found his secret places....

This woman is now dead leaving Ayurzana Luvsandamba to prepare
for death alone in Ulaanbaatar, a city she had never known.
                                   ...Death is different here
but he will reject meat and strong drink, shave his head:
                                            ...keep to the old ways.

It isn't

    the unwavering concentration on the screen,
the regurgitation of appointments, follow-ups ,scans,
diagnoses, interpretation of results in a language
resonating familiarity within the ears yet is still

evasive, not fully understood no matter how often
one resorts to the concise O. E. D. or, yes,
understood linguistically but not the full import,
full impact, the diminution of days, concertina-ed

days, goals; nor is it the ameliorating response
to that question you have so carefully, so lightly,
led up to, the one that achieves the determined
swivel of the consultant's chair and defies his eye,

 elicits his practised, oil-voiced proclamation
…individual assessment of each individual case…
yet makes no further appointment but stands,
shakes your hand firmly declaring his intention

to write immediately to your G.P. No. This you can ignore,
these are minor indications. It is when the G.P. levels,
at last, with the 'good news' of chocolate and cheese,
and yes! The benefits of a second, or more, glass of wine….

For Mary

i.m. Mary MacRae

Dusty brown or lucent
white breasting high cliffs
perhaps a flash of blue
the eye's gleam caught
recorded, given voice.

Between the reading
and the comments
we wait for your voice
in silence we miss you
as birds do*.

---

* Mary MacRae's first collection was *As Bird's Do*.

Bury your own dead

Do not ask me to bury your dead,
to pitch earth where worms sidle
amongst the ash and gob of him
whose drink-palsied hands clung
to the shovel, his sweat scalding
the mud and suck of a grief-hole
for one he never knew nor cared.

I'll not be there in mirrored shades
displaying loss in some false array
of plucked flowers, another's artifice
weaving wire through stems to form
a name so common the florist keeps
frames ready made but who agrees
grief that is so precious has no price.

You will not see me shadowing wall
or pew, black merged with black, hat
low, cuffing a tear, mourning her life.
I will not sit silent for false moments
recalling her laughter, compassion
or love. Do not ask me. I will remain
in our room holding her empty glove.

What is left

    is distance: the bald-headed eagle
quartering the land, seeking below amongst
rough tussocks for scut of rabbit, dispersion
too late as shadow and claw blot out the sun
where once Icarus soared and he, also, fell,
perhaps on such an evening as other lovers
flattened this very heather, these tall grasses
glowing purple-yellow, bruising the light. Now,
they stand proud: a magpie pecks, desultory.

Perspective

It is February. From the tracks beyond the cemetery
the last train defies the dark, defies the dark

beyond the cemetery. It is February. Onto the tracks
a body may fall, fall from the bridge

the bridge that springs over the tracks, the tracks
on which a body may span, horizontal

east to west or west to east, never north to south
south to north. Horizontal.

Too late, too late to grind the brakes, the brakes
too late if a body breaks on the tracks.

The woman at the window sees the man on the bridge
to the man on the bridge the woman at the window cries
                                              Wait.

Spanning the tracks that the driver can see
but not a body spanning the tracks

there is no body spanning the tracks as he moves on,
moves on defying the dark

beyond the cemetery. It is February. The rails are sharp
the night is clear, he is on time.

The driver's on time. All is ordered in this dark. He's taken advice.
He can implement procedures. Procedures.

Vera climbs the stairs of the bridge, sees the man on the bridge
hears the cry of the woman at the window but not the word.
                                            She is alone.

He cuts a swathe towards the tunnel. He is on time
he is a man who defies the dark

he is a man moving on, moving on through the night
the night is ordered, he is ordered

the driver's on time. He's taken advice. He keeps his hand
he stays his hand, he can implement…

The boy sleeping under the bridge hears slippers shuffling
the bridge hears a woman's cry. He doesn't move. It could be
a ploy.

Procedures. He knows procedures. He knows this track.
He knows the exact, the exact point

to release, to release pressure. The driver's taken advice.
The air is clear. The rails are sharp. He is a man defying the dark.

The man on the bridge hears the train on the track, hears a voice calling,
footsteps dragging. He turns. She is cardigan-ed not white-coated.
Disguised.

It is February. The air is clear. They are beyond the cemetery.
Beyond fear. The fear on the face of the man in the train of the man
in the air.

North Circular

It was always there, the face, the wrench of wheel,
the way the skid tapered into the tree, the gape
of door with the one arm hanging loose and him
– not waiting for the familiar wail, familiar questions –
exploding onto the tarmac, trainers pumping black,
a race with more than a medal or gold cup to win.

O'Shea Is Granted Enlightenment Outside Fantasy Nails, Boston, Massachusetts

Simultaneously diminutive and bold, its glue seeping
onto the glass of the salon door from the day's heat,
he'd flicked a glance at it, handwritten, before shrugging
to the subway but intrigued, retraced his steps to re-read

No soliCiTOrs alloWed In SalLon.

Such discrimination against one profession? Had the conveyancer
proved rogue? Left the new owner bereft, bounced cheques,
unmet debts? Or was it a warning to a lover? Husband suspects....
Or a code to a coke king? Had the cops the place cased? Or? Or...?

Pursued by scenarios he walked the Freedom Trail, hopped-on
hopped-off the Trolley Tour, took the trip around the harbour
re-fuelling at Finagle Bagel, swerved panhandlers and punks,
touting bartenders, camera-toting tourists, street performers

on every corner till midnight when he flopped from the T, tacked
down Mass. Av. on blistered feet to stand before that irregular line,
the salon now dark, the street empty though by the scrubby park
cigarettes were proffered, lights flickered, a woman's shadow
detached itself and a voice, smooth as molasses, sang in his ear,

Whatsa big boy like you doin' here? Wanna try for a night flight?

Histories

Narrative

Narrative? There is no narrative. Unless you mean
the mice-scratch of voices rising from the reeds'

silty bed or the latent lick of water rimming the bank
from a rower already beyond the curve of the river.

Yet ever, as the last harsh of the late returning crow,
deep-locked, shackles the evening, there remains,

unresolved but latched in re-arrangements of light, air,
stealth, in a conspiracy of shadows, such a hunger

for the unremembered that even a midge or squall of dust
recalls maps of countries no longer named and those

who have no purchase trace, with naked eye, the plane's
arc prinked in the sky like stars in a child's colouring book.

Vasilije: Christmas Eve

He skirled towards me, a rasp and hawk of a man,
his mouth adrift in his face. He volleyed forth words

repeated over and over whilst inquisiting the shifting sky
the way you seek beyond the fluencies of light,

uncertainties inherent in the night's sequence:
the way shepherds scoured hills, on guard against wolves,

only to be ambushed by a hustle of angels,
by hallelujah upon hallelujah flinching still air

and that one star that even now hovers, uncertain,
above those precious wild words.

Josif

Beyond the window — glass, plate —
the clack and stubble of Monday

where pavements flow an oil-slick
of workers who gallopade, glissade

side-step, smile apologies. Behind him,
his faithful Gaggia infuses a keep-heat mug

in a rage of steam, its screech a rival
to the planes that once coiled his valley,

strafing the grey-green haze of olives,
eclipsing the cries of cicadas in the long grass

— him already knowing only the male shrieked —
as he huggled within the reek of his father's thin body.

Josif knows now from that particular clunk-k-k
that his old friend is close to serving his last.

He prays they will struggle through this lunch.
Placing a biscuit beside the cappuccino

he shumbles towards the glass-topped table
too soon finger-smeared, grieves the passing

of easy-wipe formica, the taking of small cups
over conversations in sunlit squares, accepts

the flicker of eye as Hvala*, contemplates
the silent elegance of a close-furled umbrella.

* Hvala Thank you

The Re-Telling

Without light we travelled, bent by snow,
the ice-bite of stars in a flinty sky our typography,
each letter conveying the weight of history:
the genesis of making the unknown, known.

    *

Steel-caps know how to make a light history. A shiver
of glass an' mate, the Lecky's *Any person damaging*...
As if we gave a flying fuck. We wanted dark. The alley.
His way home. No way out. He'd pay. He'd know

Don't mess with Joe. Mean. Joe's been with that Mary
a coupla years an' not even dipped his wick. Not bent.
Says in his country a wife comes pure. Virgin. Spotless
Not even thought about it. Thank Christ I live here.

    *

We were reluctant to leave. One said the stars were out
of alignment, the second spoke of our other false hopes.
And why leave my new concubine who would weave
intricate patterns on my skin she'd cooled with rose water,
her hennaed fingers, such a pale shade of brown, feeding
me only the finest figs, first drawing that glistening purse
bursting with seed into her own mouth to moisten before
flicking it on her tongue...Such a tongue. The promise!
The delights to come resonating on its pink tip fluttering
between her lips, those childish lips reddened with passion.

    *

Joe's no mincer. Only gotta shake his curls an' the women...
Let's just say they were never girls. Take that first night.
Sight of 'em hunched over his lunch pack. Talk about
share and share alike. None of 'em 've looked back since.

An' the mouths on 'em. They notch up scores in the carsie.
That Mary'll never know. Never see her. Old man keeps her
tighter 'n a duck's arse. 'Cept for Joe. Sundays. Saint's days.
Nutty things like that. He's there. I swear, butter wouldn't melt....

We get a look in then. Not that Joe's lairy with it. No way. Knows.
Show respect or pay. That fairy Gabe'll find out. Don't mess
with a bloke's tart. He shoulda kept to Teresa. Mother Teresa.
She's all heart. Six kids, dozen dads. An' what she does for afters!

  *

But this child would be different. The crow's feather laid at each
of our doors, not once but each of three nights, the way the wind
sprang around our palaces yet stilled whenever we ventured out
to consult the stars and the very stars themselves shut their faces,
ceding the desert to the ululations of wolves, whinny of stallions,
their wild manes streaming in terror at the unexpected dark –
yes, we knew. Yet still we refused. Preferred our own pursuits.
But at the failing of all light in the Holy Place and an unknown
peacock, tail ablaze, strutted back and forth before our faces –
we were afraid. To have delayed further would betoken death.
Whose death none could say and none had words as we loaded
camels with oil and grain and gifts. Such gifts. Gifts fit for a King.

  *

Mean. Joe's not from round here. Being foreign. Not a turban! Just...
Foreign. But knows to keep stumm when Harold jus'-call-me-god
comes sniffing 'n' I'm off the job. I've a nice little earner on the side.
Not been rumbled. Though Joe's got a whiff. But no lip, just covers.
And he's a good chippy. So. This little number's a *Thanks, Joe*.

Mel gave me me blade. Nice. Jag-edged. Serrated. Got it in Ibiza.
He'd had a ruck with a coupla local gits. You don't fuck with Mel.
They hopped it fast as a fart in a colander. Left this. See. It glints.
Gold. Gabe'll appreciate it. Or maybe not. Won't be singing then.
Not if we give him a little cut where he wouldn't show his mother.

Yeah. Little nick there…Be well good. Being what he's done to Joe.
Choir. 'S how Gabe latched onto Mary. So it's only fair we help him
with high notes. Voice like an angel. Posh talk. Posh job. Newsreader.
Trainee. Thatch of blonde hair. Him not her. Got her dad to let him
walk her home nights Joe was … whatever. So reckon we need
to give him something to sing about over the hills and far away.

*

Yes, the journey was hard and often we were quarrelsome,
resenting the loss of our independence in the governance
of our days. We cleansed our selves once, twice, thrice daily
yet still the sand penetrated our robes, hid in the folds of skin
within our innermost parts, our buttocks rubbing sore against
each jolt of camel and the camels themselves, so fractious,
their beautiful eyes plagued by flies, stings suppurating belly,
back, fetlock – it was torture to shackle them during the day
as we slept. Their spit grew venomous. Our words likewise.
Yet we knew each man's wisdom complemented the others'.
We knew also to seek inner solitude in this crowded desert.

*

I've kept well stumm about this little caper. Mel knows. An' Balfy.
His aftershave! Ruddy corpse long dead an' dug up smells sweeter.
Umbelliferous plant, my eye. If his smell gives this rumble away.…
Mind. He's an answer for everything. Reckons what I use to calm
me nerves causes me asthma, makes me gasp, so he calls me.
Gasper. He gets sarky, I get narky. But come something like this.…
Like brothers. Never mind being mob-handed. Leave that to the rest.
Come the acid test, we're there for each other. We stick like shit.
We all operate our own patch. Our own little kingdom. Our own tarts.
Keep our selves to selves. But when its curtains you call for mates
you can rely on for certain. An' that's Mel. An' me. An' Balfy. Natch.

*

Yet when we were greeted by horseman we drew together as one.
We waited silently. No steel was drawn. We did not possess such.
Our wisdom serves as our weapon. Oh, had we had the wisdom
to refuse the press of these strangers, to choose another direction,

to keep our news close, we would have been spared the ignominy
history has imposed upon us. But I plead, what choice did we have?
Our reputation in the reading of stars had preceded us, the horseman
inviting participation in the delights of the palace were quietly forceful.
After the itch and scratch of desert fleas it seemed sanctuary indeed.
But, in mitigation, know we refused to partake of the king's concubines.

*

Then there's Harold's lot. Does the dirty work for the Eye-ties.
Well geared up. Big knives, small pricks. You keep that stumm!
He'd give me a right bum's rush faster'n you can flick a bogey –
gotta think of me day job. The legit one. I'm no layabout. No way!
Work hard, play hard. Two jobs. And a little night earner with girls.
Till the Eye-ties muscled in. They know how to flank 'emselves
over the manor. Each protecting the other's fanny. Friggin' pain.
They came, fought, set up a chain of command an' moved on.
Harold's their main man here. His business is just a front! Clever!
Ever want to slit your own throat, step out of line. He'll do it for you.
Legit. You'll never work again. He calls the union his army. The git!

*

The star led us to him who would be known King of the Jews.
Others were present. Each paying his dues. The mother shed
the same remote smile on shepherd or goat, camel or king.
Afraid we had been followed we laid our gold, frankincense
and myrrh, made our obeisance and sought another direction
to our land which gave us succour. We will not travel again.

*

Where's that ponce Gabe gone? Bloody choir's well over. He shows
it'll be his ruddy swan song. Reckon he's heard about Joe's bird. Knows
we know who's been walking her home, Sweet talking when she's alone.
The word'll be out on the street we're waitin'. There's no escaping that.
'S a fact of life round here. Eyes out of their backsides some of 'em.
I swear they're aware of every fart or fuck before it's even started.

Too friggin' scared to do anything. Look at that ruck yesterday. It was Harold's mob. He heard on the grapevine about some geezer marking his territory. So he puts out feelers. These three likely lads They harp on they know what's what. He treats 'em royally. Booze, birds, blokes, the lot. That was as far as he got. How thick can you be? Right prick. First opportunity they scarpered. Left Harold carping.

He's not one to take things lying down but even for him it was over the top. He had his spies out day an' night, non-stop. Spies know. They wanna live they've gotta come up with the info. Any info. Fast. So they did. Why they chose that actual neighbourhood? Suppose… they wanted rid. Harold off their backs. An' he didn't hang around. Swore he'd gun the geezer wherever. But Christ! A kid's playground!

Aftermath

Beside the cup, the saucer. White. Plain. Not even
a silver edging the rim. The tea she takes is herbal,
camomile, vanilla and honey gently infusing the air.

The hand is steady, pale, the long fingers broken,
nail-less. Our eyes try not to register this. Or her mouth.
She adapts her twisted lips to the angle of rim,

her fingers to its changing weight. It soothes. The voice
is melodious. Incongruous. She pats the flab of stomach
disproportionate to her frame, to the curve of calf, slender

thighs that meet the overhang of flesh. *Bar-ren*. She shrugs.
Her eyes hold history. *What good grudge?* Sliced syllables,
inverted words, language constructed for ease of that mouth,

are interrupted by her one waiter who remained. He places
a clumped hand on the once-silk shoulder, takes our order.
Our stutter of French barely comprehensible but not guttural.

The *frites* come heaped under a lidded salver, laid with flourish
on the red-white check by steak, thin, aroma-wrapped in garlic.
Eat, she said, *Eat*. And pushed towards us all her deprivation.

Appetites

Wheeling on a fish-wind, an orchestra of gulls
claw the sunless sky, scavenge for offal thrown,

careless, upon a wind that will change direction,
pitting sand into skin, into the over-ripe fruit

of a white-fleshed peach the woman savours; juice
weeping over that marginal place of the heart.

Ghazal

If you sing off-key about a certain smile
and croak across the table my eyes beguile,
                    should I presume?

Or when I admire some other man's profile
you deride his hair, shirt, shoes, his very style –
                    should I presume?

Then you flirt with dusky Sasha – young, nubile –
dance, flay your arms to prove that you're still virile
                    should I presume?

And when you say with passion all love's puerile
cows eyes and sighs should be banished, exiled
                    should I presume?

If then you tease, smile, seek to please, reconcile,
send white wine with almond blossom – so fragile!
                    should I presume?

Neve! But if, while you're reading Proust or Carlyle,
you let me rock to the Stones, sing to Kurt Weill
                    should I presume?

Ghazal: In Situ

She was where where she always longed to be, in situ:
ecstatic that every one could see she's in situ

Such hunger creates its own incontinence:
penchants pursued, captured, remain inexorably in situ.

Displacement and/or dispersal results in diaspora
so is it now only the refugee in situ?

Once it was beads that bought land or love
but times are harder so what's bartered? Bodies: in situ.

The well-groomed lover picks a speck from his coat, proffers
proposal, offer rejected, scratches his head: a chimpanzee in situ?

Heads tumbled from tumbrels for liberté, fraternité, egalité
but now with the Marquis dead it is the bourgeoisie in situ.

In truth I lost my head when you softly whispered my name,
did not know love was a game played simply in situ.

Black Bandanna

The woman in the black bandanna refuses
the offer of an arm to cross from Harvey Nic's
slewing her eyes on the black booted beauty
who clicks between the traffic's mesh, trips
the station's steps to escalate underground.

The woman in the black bandanna, uncertain
in a certain light, draws back, gathers a scruff
of astrakhan close to slackened neck, watches
for the wink of red to halt snarling taxis, hears
the gathering rumble of the train underground.

The Collection

She passed from house to house, the black bag
on her wrist slack, sucked in, its cloth well-worn
from years of visitings, a witness to all passings.

Hand raised, face set to subdued, she'd execute
a respectful knock, step back, listen for a shuffle
of slippered feet, the intake of breath at a squeeze

past the pram in the passage, the click of the latch.
Into the sliver of light behind the door she'd deliver
her hushed naming, patiently wait whilst the purse

was fetched, avert her eyes as a coin, its value giving
the nearness of neighbour, was dropped into the bag.
She'd murmur the appropriate words before allowing

the luxury of the turning over of a long life long known
to all. Some say such honour was not rightfully hers,
having no birth ties in the street but only arriving aged

five years, the rest of her family having now moved on.
Others swear seeing her following the late Mrs. Copage,
the eldest of the street's oldest family, who held the bag

at that time, shaping her child-mouth in the same way,
leaving with the same sorrowful look, her wrist curved
as if the weight of future coinage already hung there.

Alterations

Light-boned she had always been easy to swing over his shoulder
his hands deep in the taffeta of her skirt, her laughter high-pitched
she kicked then danced the air whilst he held her triumphant, aware.

        Aware, whilst he held her triumphant,
           she kicked then danced the air.
        She had always been easy, a swinger,
           had always looked over his shoulder.
        His knife deep in the taffeta of her skirt,
           her voice high-pitched, she was light.
                  Boned

Acceptance

As a window, curtained with the night's dark
shields the day

Or a man's face, lathered, hides each line
his father bore

Or pools of lamplight distances fear between
midnight's measured steps

So each thankful closing of crumpled eyelids
holds its own covenant.

On Our 60th Anniversary

Unlaced shoes slither entrails
of black, a last button discards
its final thread leaving belly
gaping in late autumn air.
Leaves heaped for the burning
shiver at the caress of wind.
In the stoop and slack of love
a thin sun warms our bones.

Histories

Behind her high bed a telephone long since
disconnected connects

                        the ragged edge
of a voice never heard in this back country

but recognised in the disgruntled *caa-caa*
when a strut of crow picks clean the husks
in a field long since harvested.

Outside,
the moon harsh, slopping its careless light
over a mesh of leaves, patterns the ground.

Subsequent

It is the long sprawl of a late summer afternoon:
the pyrocanthus prickling the wall has not yet

the redness of berries nor white of flower
but bears a glint as a solitary finch pulses

the hours: the light lean in the tangle where thicket
smothers detail whilst absence smirrs

the first throat of darkness, dismantling the margins,
and grief's half-light leaves one beyond self.

Autumn will come soon over the mountains
bringing a thunder of flies with small stings.

Dismantling the Margins

Shaping the poem

And as you sit in silence behind the closed door does the vagrant word edge past, creep between lintel and jamb, evade the grasping pen and group into iambs you never sought? Does a cry of anguish from unmarked paper fill the room, batter the walls, or is it smothered by curtains always drawn against the marauding light that will fade each character so desperately wrought?

Punctuation

She needed
        something
to punctuate the day

between the (
and forward /
    of life.

a , maybe
       or the shift
to an '

distinguishing the
       abbreviation
from the possessive.

She marks it with a little
       flirtation
perhaps an excited   !

but she'll never go
       the whole way
and avoids the   .

Although she will accomodate
       the meaningful pause
The   … moment.

Investigate

this
it is not
in
definite
rather the
con
verse
converse with
this
[A.-S. thes, fem. theos, neut. this]
(cp. Dut. deze, Icel. thessi)
this
denotes
implies
familiar
it can be said therefore with
con
tempt
would you say it with contempt?
would you say
this
with contempt?
would you say this?
would you say
con…
would you tempt
this
would you?

no t e
the frailty
of
this
it is
cognisant with
that

the
or fellow gang members
these.
does this
alone
diminish him to
subject his status to
the definite in definite?
he is a subrogate as a
pro noun
for the definite
article
say table
la table (fem) der Tisch (masc)
except in
chinese
zhuMźi
(ch. romanization no in / definite articles)

this
is an exception

this may also be used to
intensify
as in
this
usually proclaimed on a rising note
which could denote
con
tempt
for the thisness of this the
hæcceity
the essential
property that

con
fers
individuality on an
individual

no te
we will not investigate
con
fers
due to
temp
oral considerations which
this
also embraces
urging
one
or more
to
in
this
invest.

What....

That little bar above
that ginger man twisting a string bag,
that little light-y thing-y, says, is
that it's Cockfosters
that this train is terminating,
that it will go no farther,
that the driver will be leaving it there.
That will be the moment
that the guard discovers
that his wife has, again, decided, determined,
that avocado and mustard sandwiches are all
that is necessary to ensure
that a man remains regular. And I bet
that you wouldn't have thought
that.
                    ...ever

Oblique. Each font to enhance specificity
where words employed denote ambition.
Lines either parallel or at right angle
indent inlay marquetry will denote skill.
Nota Bene: notes kill if words merge
or add factor r to see banker run loss
one jumps to the gun another simply jumps.

Coalition denotes deconstruction of particles part-icles p-articles policy articles artic-u-lated in previous part-y machine output adhered slavishly by ingrates overlooking Abraham's de-selection of son for thicket lamb organic to manifesto-manifestations from on high i.e. a burning Bush – long may he suffer – erstwhile noting conflagration is resultant upon substitution of truth that does not, should not, will not take capital theft as the prerogative of aforesaid command structure which if not singular denotes fusion precedes chaos.

Concentration of focus on farrow reveals substantial presence of activated masses reproducible in the private/public/space/arena. Reference to and intelligent awareness surrounding such fuscous environs in which the above trajectories frequently occur will create resistance to those conditions associated within the labyrinth which, heretofore, necessitated ontological consultation.

Prolonged passage prior to ejection signals reluctance to vacate the private space for public arena preferring to engage solely within known matter. Such eloquent, albeit unspoken, commitment demonstrates an unconscious denial regarding an over-arching universal omniscience with the right to self-determination remaining inviolate. Q.E.D.

from *Unto Us A Pig Is Born*

To Whom It May Concern

Correspondence is the extradition of thought-word to known/unknown destination rendering prospective associative factors to be instigated e.g. wood board water waterboard dead deadwood dead-in - wood dead would assist elasticity retaining assertive phonemic migration to projective usage in performative territory, the integral process necessitating structural rationale, including machinations of authorial intervention, applying kinetic force, polemic discursive, self-referential avoidance, possibly cryptic parataxis.
      I shall never write to you again.

RUTH O'CALLAGHAN has five collections of poetry, has been translated into six languages and is much anthologised. Invited to read throughout Asia, Europe, and the U.S.A., she was awarded a gold medal for poetry at the XXX WCP in Taiwan. The Arts Council of England sponsored her visit to Mongolia to collaborate with women poets and this resulted in a book and a CD. She holds the prestigious Hawthornden Fellowship and was nominated for the Pushcart Prize. She is a mentor and workshop leader both in the U.K and abroad. As a reviewer and interviewer she has interviewed some of the most eminent women poets throughout the world. An international competition adjudicator and editor, she is also a judge for the Koestler whose awards encourage prisoners to participate in the Arts. She hosts two poetry venues in London – the revenue from these events support three Cold Weather Shelters. She is also the poet for Strandlines, a community, multi-disciplinary project run under the auspices of Kings College, University of London.